W9-CIQ-891

How To Convince Your Parents You Can...

Care For A Pet Parrot

Amelia LaRoche

Mitchell Lane
PUBLISHERS

P.O. Box 196
Hockessin, Delaware 19707
Visit us on the web: www.mitchelllane.com
Comments? email us: mitchelllane@mitchelllane.com

Mitchell Lane
PUBLISHERS

Printing   1   2   3   4   5   6   7   8   9

A Robbie Reader/How to Convince Your Parents You Can...

Care for a Kitten
Care for a Pet Bunny
Care for a Pet Chameleon
Care for a Pet Chimpanzee
Care for a Pet Chinchilla
Care for a Pet Ferret
Care for a Pet Guinea Pig
Care for a Pet Hamster
Care for a Pet Hedgehog
Care for a Pet Horse

Care for a Pet Mouse
Care for a Pet Parrot
Care for a Pet Racing Pigeon
Care for a Pet Snake
Care for a Pet Sugar Glider
Care for a Pet Tarantula
Care for a Pet Wolfdog
Care for a Potbellied Pig
Care for a Puppy
Care for a Wild Chincoteague Pony

Library of Congress Cataloging-in-Publication Data
LaRoche, Amelia.
    Care for a pet parrot / by Amelia LaRoche.
        p. cm. — (A Robbie reader. How to convince your parents you can—)
    Includes bibliographical references and index.
    ISBN 978-1-58415-795-3 (library bound)
    1. Parrots—Juvenile literature. I. Title. II. Title: How to convince your parents you can—care for a pet parrot.
     SF473.P3L37 2010
     636.6'865—dc22
                                                                                          2009004523

ON THE COVER: Front—Eclectus; insets—Budgerigar (left), Blue-fronted Amazon; Back—Lovebirds

ABOUT THE AUTHOR: Amelia LaRoche lives in New England with three wonderful parrots. (Her fourth passed away in 2009 and is missed by the entire flock—human and avian.) Her later parrots were adopted, but she bought her first one from a unique store where she ended up working for a short time. The owner cared deeply for birds, and he wrote a comprehensive list letting people know how challenging it is to have a pet parrot. However, no list—or book—can truly prepare anyone for daily life with a parrot. LaRoche believes parrots are meant to live in their natural environment, and that those in captivity should be given the best lives possible. She hopes future parrot owners will opt for adoption, and that everyone will donate money or time to a rescue organization like Foster Parrots or Project Perry Inc.—The Central Virginia Parrot Sanctuary. Both groups have the dual mission of rescuing captive parrots and protecting parrots in the wild.

PUBLISHER'S NOTE: The facts on which this story is based have been thoroughly researched. Documentation of such research is listed on page 29. While every possible effort has been made to ensure accuracy, the publisher will not assume liability for damages caused by inaccuracies in the data, and makes no warranty on the accuracy of the information contained herein.

PLB

TABLE OF CONTENTS

Words in **bold** type can be found in the glossary.

Jardine's parrot

Macaws are native to South and Central America and Mexico and come in all sizes. One of the most popular pet macaws is the Blue-and-Gold, which can live for up to seventy years. Their naked cheeks "blush" when they are excited.

 Chapter One

A PET THAT SAYS, "I LOVE YOU!"

Parrots are amazing animals. They can talk, laugh, dance, and fly. You can even teach them tricks—like putting a ball in a hoop, meowing like a kitten, or roller skating across the floor.

Parrots have colorful feathers. They have shiny, intelligent eyes with pupils that "pin," or quickly go from large to small, when they are excited. They can hold toys and food with their feet.

Wouldn't it be fun to live with a pet that can mimic the sound of a ringing telephone, a beeping microwave oven, and your own voice? Few other pets can say, "I love you!"

These intelligent creatures can be the most entertaining pet you will ever have. Your entire family might enjoy laughing at the antics of a friendly budgerigar (BUD-jur-ee-gar), cockatiel, or Quaker parakeet that hangs upside down from your finger or whistles a joyous tune.

Even small budgerigars can get into big trouble! Always supervise your parrot when it is enjoying its daily out-of-cage time.

You should know something else. Parrots are very loud, very messy, and sometimes very **destructive**. Most of all, they are very needy. They can scream so loudly and chatter so much, you'll wonder why you ever wanted a parrot. They fling their food all over their cages and onto the floor. They chew expensive furniture. They poop on clothes and break buttons in half with their beaks. Some will never learn to talk, and most will only learn a few words. It takes huge amounts of time and patience to teach parrots tricks. Worst of all, parrots sometimes bite . . . *hard!* Because many types of parrots live for so long, they can be a lifetime pet. A lifetime is a *long* time.

Parrots are not **domesticated** animals, like dogs and cats. Even parrots bred in **captivity** are still wild at heart. They are very smart because in their natural

habitats they must solve a lot of big problems— like where to find food in which season, how to choose a nest, how to raise babies and teach them all they need to know, how to get away from **predators** on the ground and in the sky, and how to get along with all the other birds in the flock.

For a parrot with a big brain and the urge to fly and raise a family, it is very hard to be stuck in a cage all day. For this reason, some experts believe parrots should not be kept as pets. If you do keep a parrot as a pet, you must work hard to make sure it has a happy life. You have to feed it a diet that takes effort to prepare. You will need to buy or make it new toys often. It will need to come out of its cage every single day for exercise and attention. Even small parrots can live for decades. After the excitement of having a new pet wears off, your parrot will still need daily care for many years. Can you promise to provide that? Not everyone can. In fact, most people can't. Parrots are not for most people.

Blue-and-Gold macaws are very loud, so they don't make good apartment or dormitory pets. These playful birds have a wingspan of about three and a half feet, so they need a big cage. This pair is enjoying natural sunlight in an outdoor aviary.

Chapter Two

BIRDS OF A FEATHER FLOCK TOGETHER

There are about 350 species of parrots. They come in every size and color you can imagine. Their habits in the wild vary widely. Most species live in tropical regions. Nearly two-thirds live in South and Central America.

ainbow lorikeet

The largest parrot is the electric-blue Hyacinth macaw of South America. This gentle giant can grow to three and a half feet. The smallest is the three-inch-long pygmy parrot of Papua, New Guinea.

Parrots live in flocks, and most mate for life. They use their loud voices to tell one another about good food or dangerous predators, such as hawks and eagles. Large macaws can be heard from miles away.

Parrots have strong, curved beaks and thick, sensitive tongues. They are great fliers. Air sacs throughout their bodies keep them light on the wing.

With many species of parrot, the only way to tell the male and female apart is by testing their DNA. An exception is the eclectus parrot. The female is red, and the green male's beak looks a little like a piece of candy corn.

They are not as graceful on the ground. They waddle when they walk! Their feet have four toes: two in front and two in back. They hold their food with their feet while they eat.

Many parrots have green **plumage**, and this lets them blend in with the treetops. Some, like Rainbow lorikeets, have many colors. Experts say these bright colors and patterns make it hard for a predator to see where the bird's body stops and starts. Even the brightest parrots are nearly invisible in their natural habitats.

Males and females usually look alike. One exception is the eclectus (ee-KLEK-tus) of Australia. The males are lime green and the females are purplish red and blue. At first, scientists watching them in the wild thought they were different species.

Parrots use many places to lay their eggs. Macaws nest high in palm trees that have been hollowed out by termites. The kakapo (KAH-kuh-poh) of New Zealand, which is the only parrot that cannot fly, nests on the ground. Several species carve holes

The kakapo is one of the world's rarest parrots, and the only flightless, nocturnal parrot. While it's not the longest, it is also the world's heaviest parrot, with some males weighing more than eight pounds. Only a handful remain in the wild.

into termite nests. Patagonian conures (KAHN-yurs) dig long tunnels in sandstone cliffs and riverbanks. African lovebirds build nests inside tree holes. The female cuts leaves and bark into strips, tucks them into her feathers, and flies them to the nest.

Female Quaker parakeet "Walter" laid this egg.

A naked baby

Though parrots come in every color, their eggs are always white. Baby parrots hatch from the egg naked. Their eyes are shut tight. At first, they eat soft food **regurgitated** (ree-GUR-jih-tay-ted) by their mother. As the chicks grow, the parents take turns feeding them. Budgerigars and lovebirds are ready to fledge, or fly from the nest, when they are about forty-five days old. African gray parrots

Most parrot species start growing feathers after a couple of weeks.

Baby African grays have dark eyes that turn yellowish in adulthood.

take about seventy days. Macaws are ninety days old before they make their first flight.

After galah (guh-LAH) parrots in Australia leave the nest, they join nursery groups that are overseen by a few adults. They practice their flying skills and learn how to behave in a flock. After many months, they are ready to set out on their own. Some birds, like African grays, stay in family flocks for years before they find their own mates.

Parrots have a long lifespan. Budgerigars live about fifteen years. Lovebirds and cockatiels live about twenty years. African grays, Amazons, and macaws can easily reach the age of fifty.

Nearly a third of all parrot species are endangered in the wild.

Young African grays are clumsy. They need to be watched carefully when they are learning to fly. Their cage floor should be padded when they are still learning to perch.

Two big threats are trapping for the pet trade and habitat loss to logging and farming.

Kabobs are a great way to serve fruits and vegetables to your parrot. You can also provide a dish for goodies your family might normally discard: fresh seeds from peppers, squash, and melons, as well as the marrow from inside cooked chicken bones. Remove all fresh food within a day so that it doesn't spoil in the cage.

 Chapter Three

GIVING A PARROT A GOOD HOME

Millions of households have pet birds. Thousands of parrots are dumped at rescues and shelters—or set loose—every year. Many are brought to shelters when a child goes to college and the parents don't want to care for the bird. Even well-loved parrots sometimes outlive their owners and become homeless.

If you are thinking about getting a parrot, first do a lot of homework. Second, make sure your parents are also eager to have a bird. That way, when you grow up and move out, if you can't bring your bird, he or she will still be loved and cared for. Third, find a parrot who needs a good home. Shelters and rescues are overflowing with them. Sometimes they are listed for a low price or "free to a good home" in the want ads.

Some people say that only baby birds make good pets, but that is not true. Adult birds are just as much

Budgerigars may be small, but they're smart! A budgerigar named Puck was accepted into the *1995 Guinness Book of World Records* as the bird with the largest vocabulary in the world. Puck spoke more than 1,700 words.

fun. Often they are more fun! Many already know how to play with toys and behave around humans.

If you volunteer at a rescue organization for a few hours a week, you will learn a lot about parrots. You will also start to get a good idea of whether having a parrot will fit your life. Many rescue organizations require volunteers to be eighteen, but some may let you accompany an adult volunteer.

If you must buy a bird instead of adopting one, choose a breeder who lets you visit his or her facility. Make sure it is clean and that the birds are well cared for. Ask a lot of questions. Good breeders will not sell you a baby until it is **weaned**. To become healthy,

well-adjusted adults, baby birds must be fully weaned and able to eat on their own before leaving their parents or the breeder. They should never be fed by inexperienced caregivers!

Your first parrot should be small and easier to handle than some of the more high-strung types. Good choices for a first bird include lovebirds and cockatiels. Budgerigars are another good choice. Most people call them "parakeets," but a parakeet is really any small parrot with a long tail and a seed-eating beak.

Look for a curious, friendly bird with bright eyes, clear nares (nostrils), and shiny feathers. Once you have selected a bird, take it to an **avian veterinarian** (AY-vee-un veh-truh-NAYR-ee-un) to have it examined and weighed. You'll then need to bring your bird to the vet every year for a checkup.

*fun*FACTS

Just like people, parrots prefer using one "hand" over the other. In a flock of conures that were studied for "footedness," half used their right foot most of the time.

Escaped pet parrots have set up colonies in many parts of the United States. Conures in San Francisco were the stars of a 2003 documentary called *The Wild Parrots of Telegraph Hill.*

Birds are social flock animals, and in the wild, they have constant company. If you get only one bird, you must be sure to give it plenty of attention every day. If you get two birds, they will keep each other company when you are not at home. Many pairs of birds that are well socialized and played with regularly love their humans as well as each other.

You will need a carry case, a portable perch or play gym, and a cage for your bird. You should buy the biggest cage you can afford. It needs to have room for plenty of toys and several perches of different widths

Parrots have excellent vision and they can see in color. Their third, clear eyelid spreads tears to keep their eyes from drying out in flight. They sometimes blink while they're bathing to keep out water, too!

and textures. Buy a square or rectangular cage that is longer than it is high. This will give your bird room to fly.

The cage also needs a mineral block and cups for water and food. You may choose to give your bird its water in a bottle. In that case, you should also give it a shallow bowl of water so that it can bathe. Bathing keeps their feathers clean and healthy. You can also use a gentle mister on your bird. Some people take their birds into the shower with them. Just don't get shampoo or soap on your bird's feathers.

Teaching a parrot tricks takes a lot of time, but when it's done with love and patience, it makes for a happier, more engaged parrot. This Green-winged macaw enjoys showing its skills on a custom-made tricycle.

 Chapter Four

LET YOUR PARROT OUT!

Before you bring your bird home, set up the cage. Choose a room where the family spends a lot of time so that your bird won't get lonely.

Clean the paper or litter at the bottom of your bird's cage every day. Wipe down perches and bars. Every couple of weeks, give the entire cage a good scrubbing with bird-safe cleanser.

Your bird needs wooden and cardboard toys that it is allowed to chew to bits. It needs feather and rope toys that it can **preen.** Include a **foraging** (FOR-uh-jing) toy in which you can hide treats, like bits of dried fruit or a couple of sunflower or safflower seeds.

Cut tree branches for the cage. Your bird will enjoy standing on these and chewing the bark. Make sure you cut branches from **"safe" trees** that are not sprayed with **pesticides.**

Different types of parrots need different diets. Learn everything you can about what is healthy for

your parrot. For most, this means a daily serving of **organic** pellets along with raw and cooked fruits, vegetables, and greens. You can also feed it nuts like almonds, filberts, and pine nuts; beans; cooked grains like brown rice; sprouts; hard-boiled eggs with the shell on; whole wheat pasta; and small amounts of chicken or other protein. An all-seed diet is not healthy for birds! Feed your bird breakfast and give it fresh water at around the same time every day. Having a routine can be comforting for your bird.

Birds should never have avocado, chocolate, pork, soda pop, very salty foods, or alcoholic beverages. Nonstick cookware should never be used around birds. The fumes will kill them. Don't use plug-in air fresheners or paint around birds.

Some people let their birds fly. Flying is natural, and it is great exercise. It makes for a happier bird. Close toilet lids and turn off the stove before you let your bird out of its cage. Cover mirrors and windows with removable decals until your bird learns that it should not fly into them. Most importantly, teach your bird to fly to you when it is called. An escaped bird is hard to catch, and it may not live long in the wild. If it is trained to come, you'll have a better chance of getting it back safely.

If you decide to have your bird's wings clipped, take it to a vet or a groomer. New feathers grow in constantly, so even a "clipped" bird may suddenly be

Take your bird outside in its cage or in a harness. The sun is good for its feathers. If you don't take your bird outside, put a **full-spectrum** light near its cage.

able to fly. It will also need to have its toenails trimmed. Never cut into the quick of the nail.

Supervise your bird during its daily time outside its cage. Don't let it near other pets. One swipe from a cat's claw can give your bird a deadly infection.

Never punish or hit your bird. Catch your bird doing what you want it to do and then praise it. If it is chewing something it shouldn't, move it to a new spot or give it an object it is allowed to chew. If it bites, put it down gently and turn away. Soon your bird will learn that when it misbehaves, you ignore it.

Cover your bird's cage at night or provide it with a snuggle tent. It will need ten to twelve hours of sleep each night.

Look at its droppings every morning when you clean the cage. Make sure they aren't watery or discolored. If your bird is always "fluffed up" and drowsy, if it starts pulling out its feathers beyond what is normal for a **molting** bird, or if it has fluid coming from its nares, take it to the vet right away.

Rotate your bird's toys often, and include one in which treats and hand-toys can be hidden. Birds should always have at least one softwood toy that they can chew to pieces. Chewing and shredding are natural behaviors for parrots, and they find them very satisfying.

Chapter Five

WILD THINGS

The closer you can make your parrot's life to what it would be like in the wild, the happier it will be.

Parrots greet each other loudly when the flock roosts at night. Greet your bird as soon as you get home from school.

Parrots preen each other's hard-to-reach spots, like the head and neck. Stroke, preen, and cuddle your bird every day. Let it preen your hair.

Many parrots mate for life. That means your parrot may become overly attached to one person in the family. Ensure that your parrot is handled and given affection by everyone in the family so that it does not become a "one-person" bird.

Chewing, foraging, and problem-solving are natural instincts for your bird. It needs daily challenges. Teach it tricks. Hide treats in its cage. Let it watch a children's television show or a DVD of parrots in the wild. Parrots love to play and shout.

Dance with it or sing along when your favorite song comes on the radio.

In the wild, parrots can fly dozens of miles daily in search of food. Pet parrots need daily out-of-cage time.

Remember, you are the head "bird" in the flock as far as your parrot is concerned. That means you must patiently teach your bird what it needs to know. Teach it to step onto your finger. Teach it to be gentle with its beak. Teach it to fly or walk to you when it is called.

Birds sometimes don't like trying new foods. Show your parrot how delicious a new food is by eating the food in front of it. You may have to offer a new food many times before your bird tries it.

Kea

Include your bird in your daily life. Let it sit on its play gym or your desk while you're doing your homework. Let it out of its cage while you're making its breakfast. Offer it a bit of apple or a grape. Give it a piece of your breakfast cereal or your toast.

Hand-feeding your parrot healthy snacks will bring you both closer. This African gray is enjoying an organically grown apple. Always wash produce carefully before feeding it to your bird.

Persuade Mom and Dad that you are much more likely to eat your vegetables if your parrot is allowed near the dinner table to try some, too! When you are watching TV or curling up to read a book, let your parrot join you.

Keep learning about your parrot by reading books and magazines, watching videos, and joining a club where you can talk to other parrot caregivers.

Having a parrot is a big responsibility. You should think long and hard before you get one. You may be able to convince your parents that you should have a

Intelligent Quaker parakeets are popular pets. Because they can build stick nests, escaped Quakers have been able to thrive in Illinois, New York, Connecticut, and other states that have freezing winters.

parrot—but you must be sure they want one, too. Now that you know what they're like and how much work they require, you also have to convince yourself that you should have a parrot! If you have even the slightest doubt, do not get one. Nothing is sadder than seeing an unhappy bird living out a long, lonely life in a cage. However, if you do give a needy parrot a new and wonderful life, nothing will sound sweeter than its call of joy when you return home and the "flock" is together again!

Books and Articles

Bonforte, Lisa. *Learning About Parrots*. Mineola, NY: Dover Publications, 2002.

Leon, Vicki. *A Rainbow of Parrots (Jean-Michel Cousteau Presents)*. Montrose, CA: London Town Press, 2006.

Rawson, Katherine. *If You Were a Parrot*. Mount Pleasant, SC: Sylvan Dell Publishing. 2007.

Tweti, Mira. *Here, There, and Everywhere: The Story of Screeeeeeeech the Lorikeet*. Playa del Rey, CA: Parrot Press, 2007.

Wexo, John Bonnett. *Parrots (Zoobooks)*. Peru, IL: Wildlife Education, Ltd., 2000.

Works Consulted

The Bird with the Largest Vocabulary in the World
http://birdwithmostwords.com/

Brightsmith, Donald. *Nest Sites of Wild Parrots*. Originally published in Bird Talk magazine, February 2000.
http://vtpb-www2.cvm.tamu.edu/brightsmith/Wild%20Parrots.htm

Carly Lu's Flight Blog
http://carlylusflightblog.com

FamilyPets.Net. *History of Parrots*. Australian Media Pty Ltd., 2001–2008. http://www.familypets.net/historyofparrots.htm

Hallander, Jane. *Flock Behavior: How It Affects Our Companion Parrots*. Originally published in The Gray Play Round Table magazine, Winter 2001.
http://www.africangrays.com/articles/behavior/flocks.htm

Heidenreich, Barbara. *The Parrot Problem Solver*. Neptune City, NJ: T.F.H. Publications, Inc., 2005.

Kelly, Denise, Eileen McCarthy, Krista Menzel, and Monica Engebretson. *Avian Welfare Issues: An Overview*. Avian Welfare Resource Center from the Avian Welfare Coalition, updated January 2007. http://www.avianwelfare.org/issues/overview.htm

Little, Perry. Aviary Connections LLC. *Parrot History*. Perching at the Ritz, 2004–2008. http://www.lperchingattheritz.com/apps/articles/default.asp?articleid=11057&columnid=1756

Lloyd, Pauline. *Parrots in Danger*. Vegan News, 2002–2003.
http://www.btinternet.com/~bury_rd/parrot.htm

The Oratrix Project.
   http://www.freeparrots.net/parrots/index.html
The Quaker Parakeet Society.
   http://qp-society.com/qpserc/quakerbodybeautiful.html
Sparks, John, with Tony Soper. *Parrots: A Natural History*. New York:
   Facts on File, 1990.

Web Addresses and Rescues
The Association of Avian Veterinarians: Find Your Local Avian
   Veterinarian http://aav.org/vet-lookup/
The Avian Welfare Coalition
   http://www.avianwelfare.org/index.htm
Birds n Ways: Safe Plants and Trees
   http://birdsnways.com/articles/plntsafe.htm
Foster Parrots Ltd.
   http://www.fosterparrots.com/
The New Century Parrot
   http://thenewcenturyparrot.blogspot.com
ParrotChronicles.com: The Online Magazine for Parrot Lovers
   http://www.parrotchronicles.com/
Parrots International: A Treasure of Parrot Information
   http://www.parrotsinternational.org/index.html
Parrots Online: Greg Glendell, Behaviorist
   http://parrotsonline.homestead.com/Home.html
Project Perry Inc.–The Central Virginia Parrot Sanctuary
   http://www.projectperry.com/
Reymeyer, Julie J. "Helping the Cause of Macaws." *Science News
   for Kids,* http://www.sciencenewsforkids.org/articles/20070321/
   Feature1.asp
World Parrot Trust
   http://www.parrots.org/

GLOSSARY

avian veterinarian (AY-vee-un veh-truh-NAYR-ee-un)—
  Bird doctor.

captivity (kap-TIV-ih-tee)—Being held to prevent escape.

destructive (dee-STRUK-tiv)—Destroying or ruining things.

domesticated (doh-MES-tih-kay-ted)—Adapted to living
  with humans.

foraging (FOR-uh-jing)—Searching for food.

full-spectrum (full SPEK-trum)—In lighting, a bulb that
  mimics sunlight.

habitats (HAA-bih-tats)—Places where animals are found in
  the wild.

molting (MOL-ting)—Shedding feathers.

organic (or-GAA-nik)—Coming from the earth. In food,
  grown without chemicals.

pesticides (PES-tih-syds)—A substance used to kill pests,
  such as weeds or insects.

plumage (PLOO-midj)—Feathers.

predators (PREH-duh-turz)—Animals that eat other
  animals.

preen (PREEN)—To groom the feathers.

regurgitated (ree-GUR-jih-tay-ted)—Spit back out of the
  mouth, such as food from a bird's crop. The crop is a
  pouch above the stomach that stores food.

"safe" trees—Trees that are believed not to be harmful to
  birds. You can find a list of safe trees and plants on the
  Internet at http://birdsnways.com/articles/plntsafe.htm.

weaned (WEEND)—Able to feed oneself.

INDEX